BRITAIN IN O

NEWARK

T I M   W A R N E R

Nottinghamshire County Council
Leisure Services

ALAN SUTTON PUBLISHING LIMITED

Alan Sutton Publishing Limited

Alan Sutton Publishing Limited
Phoenix Mill · Far Thrupp · Stroud
Gloucestershire · GL5 2BU

First published 1995 in collaboration with
Nottinghamshire County Council, Leisure
Services Department

Copyright © Tim Warner, 1995

Cover photographs: (front) Newark May
Fair in the Market Place, *c.* 1911; (back)
Charles Street Wesleyan School's elaborate
float at a Sunday School parade, early

British Library Cataloguing in Publication Data.
A catalogue record for this book is available from
the British Library.

ISBN 0-7509-0788-6

Typeset in 9/10 Sabon.
Typesetting and origination by
Alan Sutton Publishing Limited.
Printed in Great Britain by
Ebenezer Baylis, Worcester.

Contents

NEWARK CASTLE

NEWARK-ON-TRENT

CLINTON ARMS HOTEL

TOWN HALL AND MARKET PLACE

KIRKGATE

THE CASTLE

SWIMMING POOL

LONDON ROAD GARDENS   L.7307

The principal sights of Newark set out on an early multi-view postcard.

Introduction

Quartered by the intersection of the Great North Road (A1) and the Roman Fosse Way (A46), lapped by the waters of two rivers and straddling the only level-crossing that carries the old Midland Railway clean across the former route of the 'Flying Scotsman', the Nottinghamshire market town of Newark-on-Trent certainly deserves its title as 'The Key to the North'. Historically Newark has always taken its importance (and, indeed, derived much of its wealth) from its favourable position at the intersection of these two major roads and its control of the first crossing point on the navigable River Trent upstream of the Humber. It is these attributes which have shaped the destiny of the town since earliest times.

The name Newark is thought to have been first used to describe the town during the eleventh century. The word is probably a corruption of 'new work', referring either to the rebuilding of the town following the Danish invasion in the mid-ninth century, or the first appearance of 'new works' in the form of town defences. The Domesday survey of 1086 certainly describes 'Neu Werc' as fortified; the first definite evidence of a castle, however, dates from the early years of the twelfth century.

Newark Castle was built by Alexander, Bishop of Lincoln and Lord of the Manor of Newark, somewhere between 1123 and 1148. Despite occupying a strong defensive position beside the Trent, the castle was not particularly intended to serve a military purpose and was, from the outset, merely a sumptuous, if fortified, palace. Little remains from that period, although the south-west tower and the fine Norman gatehouse of about 1170 – the finest such gatehouse in England – may still be seen.

Newark was an important garrison in the Civil War (1642–46) with the castle playing a central role in the defence of the town. Throughout the conflict Newark remained staunchly loyal to Charles I and withstood three bitter and prolonged sieges by the Parliamentary rebels. The town was never actually taken by the besiegers and only surrendered on direct orders from the king. It was on 8 May 1646 that the town's military governor, Lord John Belasis, ordered his troops to lay down their arms. He then led his garrison as they marched out of the town with full military honours before surrendering their arms to the Parliamentarians camped outside.

Following the surrender, the Parliamentary commanders ordered that the castle be torn down to prevent it ever again forming a defensive bastion within the town. That the destruction was duly started is made evident by the present gutted state of the remains, although the local residents (who were commandeered to effect the demolition) were so depleted by siege casualties

Kirkgate. To the left is what is now the King Charles Coffee House. The former Nottingham and Notts bank (furthest from the camera) was designed by the Nottingham architect Watson Fothergill; it opened in 1887. The bank is now the town's violin school.

and malnutrition that the job was never completed.

Although the castle is perhaps the most prominent landmark in Newark there are many others which, albeit less dramatically, speak of the town's past. In the south-east corner of the Market Place stands the old White Hart Inn (now a branch of the Nottingham Building Society), held to be one of the finest examples of late fifteenth-century timber-framed domestic building in England. Across the market square stands the magnificent church of St Mary Magdalene, its stone tower and spire constructed with the aid of six sturdy oaks from Sherwood Forest, granted to the town by Henry III. On the south side of the Market Place stand two former coaching inns, the Clinton Arms and the Saracen's Head. Their wide arches are now used by shoppers making their way to the modern St Mark's precinct, but once resounded with the sound of horses' hooves and iron-tyred wheels. Newark was a staging post on the London–York coach route along the Great North Road and the Clinton Arms once had stabling for no fewer than ninety horses.

It was at the Clinton Arms (then known as the Kingston Arms) that the poet Lord Byron is said to have stayed while his first two volumes of poetry (*Hours of Idleness*, 1806 and *Fugitive Pieces*, 1808) were printed across the square in the bookshop of S. & J. Ridge (now G.H. Porter's grocery shop). Twenty or so years later the Clinton played host to another famous guest, William Ewart Gladstone, who later became prime minister. Aged only twenty-two, Gladstone arrived in Newark in 1832 to fight his first election as candidate of the Duke of Newcastle. He was duly returned as the town's MP.

The wealth of Newark increased greatly during the eighteenth century as tanning, milling and brewing all became important trades. Wool, malt and malting were to follow and all benefited from the opening of the Newark Navigation in 1773. In that year too the Town Hall was begun, in fashionable Palladian style, by the noted architect John Carr of York. It was a further reflection of the town's increasing prosperity. The recently restored ballroom in the Adam style is a joy to behold.

The nineteenth century saw Newark consolidate its wealth with the expansion of the malt trade (to a point where it became the town's single most important export) together with a growth in heavy engineering. The latter was particularly connected with agricultural machinery serving the town's large agrarian hinterland. This continued prosperity is reflected in the wealth of Victorian public building spread around the town. The Corn Exchange and Gilstrap Free Library (both on Castlegate) date from 1848 and 1883 respectively, while the Ossington Coffee Palace on Beastmarket Hill was erected in 1882.

It was in the late nineteenth century that the town, with its wealth of historic buildings, began to attract the attention of pioneer photographers. The first reference to a photographer practising in the town appears in a trade directory of 1864 when James Oman of Appletongate advertised his services as Artist Photographer. By 1869 Oman had been joined by Samuel Frost of 6 Kirkgate and John McLeod whose studio address is given as Trent Bridge. Between 1869 and 1897 the number of professional photographers registered in Newark remained constant at three, the town apparently being unable to support any more. In January 1897, however, the *Newark Advertiser* announced the formation of a camera club for amateurs with no less a person than the mayor being elected as president. A second club, this time in association with the local Mechanics' Institute, was begun in 1900 and, from that time onwards, photography as a hobby appears to have enjoyed a surge in popularity. Many principal buildings and civic events received their first photographic exposure.

Over and above the trade in formal portraits and family groups, which made up the bread-and-butter business of many early photographers, it was Newark's eventful past, particularly as embodied in its historic buildings, which inspired the majority of early *plein-air* studies. Views of the castle, church, river and the town's other important buildings abound, being reproduced in quantity by the town's leading postcard manufacturers, Samuel Whiles of Stodman Street, Henry Davage of Kirkgate and Frank Robinson of Lombard Street. Taken as a whole these cards provide a fascinating record of the changing face of Newark in the early years of this century and are well represented in this book. Elsewhere I have endeavoured to include many unpublished personal photographs gathered from local residents which, set against the commercially produced postcards, provide a more intimate insight into town life. To those many individuals who, through their generosity and assistance have allowed me access to their private collections, I extend my sincere thanks. Without their help this glimpse of Newark in times past would not have been possible.

Tim Warner
March 1995

THE MARKET PLACE

Newark Market Place has always been at the heart of the town's retail trade. This section takes you on a walk around the Market Place of days gone by and looks at some of the well-remembered shops that were once located there.

The Market Place, 1850s. The engraving is taken from Thomas Bailey's *Annals of Nottinghamshire, Volume 1*. Very little has changed to this day.

In 1900 the south-west corner of the Market Place was occupied by Samuel Smith's bank. This building (centre), which also housed the County Fire Office, was demolished in 1903 to make way for that currently housing the NatWest bank.

Town Hall, west side of the Market Place. The Town Hall was built by John Carr of York and commenced in 1773. The borough police headquarters was located in the right-hand wing until 1947.

The Market Place, c. 1776. Although the Town Hall (left) was designed with classic symmetry, this engraving by E. Eyre shows the problems encountered in buying up surrounding properties to achieve the desired effect. The left-hand wing could not be completed until a number of years after the rest of the building.

The Butter Market, 1983. Beneath the Town Hall lies the Butter Market. The strong, stone pillars supporting the ballroom above also helped to keep the Butter Market cool, prolonging the life of the dairy products being sold there. The Butter Market has recently undergone major redevelopment to create a new shopping centre for the town.

The mayor's parlour, 1983. It is one of the principal non-public rooms in the Town Hall and overlooks the Market Place.

The Town Hall ballroom. Situated above the Butter Market, it is decorated in a provincial manner after the style of Robert Adam.

The Market Hall, *c.* 1890. Behind the Town Hall, leading through to Middlegate, is the Market Hall. It was constructed in 1884 at a cost of £2,500 on the site of the former butchers' shambles. The engraving shows the original sliding doors at the Middlegate end.

The Market Hall, F.M. Dawson's bookstall, 1940s.

The Market Hall, 1983. Shortly after this date it was closed and converted to shop units. For a time it was renamed the Royal Exchange, although the inappropriateness of this has since been recognized.

Cherrington's chemist shop. There has been a chemist shop on the site to the right of the Town Hall since at least the mid-eighteenth century. After 1898 it was known as Cherrington's and continued as such until as recently as April 1994. It is now Brown's the opticians.

Cherrington's chemist shop, 1954. Tom Healey is serving behind the counter.

Before George Cherrington took over sole proprietorship of the chemist shop at 5 Market Place, it was owned by Frederick March. Here March is pictured with some of his staff in the mid-1880s.

Madame Cooke's. Proceeding further along the western flank of the Market Place we cross Chain Lane and come to the shop of Madame Cooke, court costumier. It was here that the more wealthy ladies of the town bought tailor-made outfits aping the latest London and Paris fashions.

The Market Place, north-west corner. Next door to Madame Cooke's was Edith Johnson, milliner (left), offering a range of fashionable headwear to accompany Madame Cooke's gowns. To the right of Miss Johnson's is the Queen's Head public house.

W.H. Ash and Son, bakers. This tiny shop stood to the right of the Queen's Head. Many older Newark residents will remember the sharp drop down the step inside the door. Today the site has been cleared to afford a walkway, known as Queen's Head Court, through to Kirkgate.

Ash's Yard, 1928. The arched entrance to the left of Ash's shop (see above) led to the rear of the Queen's Head but was generally known as Ash's Yard. The timber-framed building seen here still stands, restored in 1960, in the present Queen's Head Court (see page 42).

Martin Wilkinson, jeweller. Jutting out into the Market Place is a group of buildings often referred to as 'Curry's block'. One of these buildings was constructed in 1885 for Martin Wilkinson, jeweller. It is currently occupied by Stephen Kettleborough, photographer.

Stennett's stationers and bookbinders. Standing at the north-west corner of the Market Place, Stennett also published the *Newark Herald* and acted as ticket agent for the Great Northern Railway. Today the building is occupied by the Leeds Building Society.

The Moot Hall, 1953. Next to Stennett's is the old Moot Hall, built in 1708. Here it houses J.H. Phillips, rope maker, and A.F. Coyne, who owned a radio and music shop. The building was taken down and entirely reconstructed in 1965–66.

A. F. COYNE

Dealer in Gramophones, Pianos and all Musical Instruments

including

JAZZ DRUMMER'S OUT-
FITS AND EFFECTS.

Complete stocks of Columbia, Zonophone and Regal Records always in stock.

Agent for the "Celebrated Clumber Gramophones."

The Reliable House for every description of Repair Work.

18 Market Place, Newark-on-Trent
Also at 48 CARTER GATE

An early trade card for A.F. Coyne's radio and music shop in the old Moot Hall. It also makes reference to their original premises, opened in the early 1920s, at 48 Cartergate.

Walter Smith's grocery shop, *c.* 1890. The shop lay to the east of the Moot Hall. Mr Smith is standing in the doorway. Piper's Penny Bazaar may be seen next door.

Building Burton's tailor's shop, north-east corner, Market Place, 1934. This afforded an unusual view of the south transept of St Mary's.

G. Winn's fish and rabbit shop. This used to form part of an extra row of buildings which lay between the church and the north side of the Market Place. It was demolished in 1892.

Small traders outside G.H. Porter's, grocery store at the north-east corner of the Market Place. Porter's is still a well-loved shop in Newark today.

Many shoppers are drawn to Porter's for their speciality cheeses and bacon, still smoked in the traditional way over oak chippings in the shop's cellar. The two pictures on this page show former owner of Porter's, Peter Spiers, beginning the smoking process.

The walls of the smoke room are lined with thick black tar – the result of over a century of constant use. Once lit, and the door closed, the fire is allowed to smoulder for up to three days to impart an inimitable flavour to the bacon hung above.

The Market Place from the Town Hall balcony, *c.* 1900. Opposite Porter's (centre left) is the shop of A.M. Matthews and Son, gentlemen's and children's outfitter, soon to be replaced by what is now the Midland Bank building.

The Arcade. At the south-east corner of the Market Place is the Arcade, leading to Cartergate. It was developed, in 1897, by Charles and Frederick Atter, managers at Bainbridges' drapery store (see pages 26–27).

WORLD RENOWNED

"NOBLE" PIES and VIENNESE BREAD

Real Vienna Dinner Rolls, 16 for 1/-

Cheerful Service

NOBLE CAFE, KIRKGATE

Pie Corner, Market Place

Tel. 366

Advertisement for Noble's Pie Corner, 1936. At the Market Place entrance to the Arcade from the 1930s to the late 1960s was Stanley Noble's Pie Corner. This advertisement incorporates a picture of Mr Noble himself.

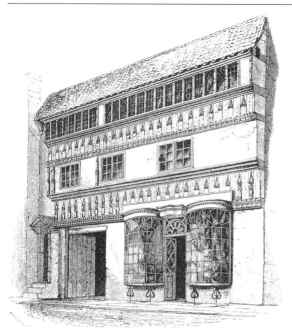

White Hart Inn, *c.* 1850. Abutting the Arcade, in the south-east corner of the Market Place, is the old White Hart, believed to have been built in about 1413.

Bainbridges' millinery department. For 101 years, between 1867 and 1968, the old White Hart building was occupied by Bainbridges' drapery shop. The almost continuous row of windows under the eaves on the third floor (see above engraving) provided plenty of natural light for Bainbridges' sempstresses and milliners.

FOR FRIENDLY
         SERVICE . . .

BAINBRIDGES (NEWARK) LTD.
General Drapers

35-39 MARKET PLACE
NEWARK
TELEPHONE: 19

Advertisement for Bainbridges, 1961. The store then occupied three buildings knocked into one. Those on the right are now occupied by W.H. Smiths.

Taylor and Son, July 1903. Within the range of buildings later occupied by Bainbridges, there once stood the shop of Taylor and Sons, chemists, and, behind it, down the passage to the right, the Blue Bell Inn. This latter was closed in 1910. In July 1903, when a colonnade still fronted these shops, a freak hailstorm smashed many windows in the town.

The Saracen's Head. Also to become part of Bainbridges, the inn dates from 1341 although this building was erected in 1721. The large central archway denotes its former role as one of Newark's eleven or so coaching inns.

Like two peas out of a Pod——

or,

INDIVIDUAL STYLE ?

TWEEDLEDUM would have looked different from Tweedledee if he'd gone to a different Tailor—then you could have recognised them apart.

Each of our suits is cut and made for the customer only—is personally fitted and perfectly finished. Your suit is made for YOU—and YOU ONLY, to fit your personality as well as your figure. In this way, individuality in style, cut, and fit is absolutely assured.

GET YOUR NEXT SUIT FROM US.

OUR CLOTHES ARE GOOD.

Johnson & Longdon

40, Market Place, NEWARK

Advertisement for Johnson & Longdon, gentlemen's outfitters, 1936 (see previous picture). They occupied part of the ground-floor range of the Saracen's Head, from as early as 1904, through to 1960 when the premises were acquired by Bainbridges.

Clinton Arms Hotel, which adjoins the Saracen's Head. It started life as the Cardinal's Hat in 1494. As with the Saracen's Head, however, the present building dates from the eighteenth century. The photograph is thought to date from May 1910, when the building was decorated for the coronation of George V.

Courtyard, Clinton Arms Hotel, 1920s. At this time the courtyard was roofed over and enclosed to form a lounge. The Clinton is noted for having been the campaign headquarters of William Ewart Gladstone when he was first elected to parliament as member for Newark in 1832.

Rear entrance, Clinton Arms Hotel, Lombard Street, 1920s. The Clinton can also claim connections with the poet Byron, who is said to have stayed at the hotel when his first poems were being printed in Newark in 1806.

Benefit Footwear, 1940s. The Public Benefit Boot Co. occupied premises beneath the Clinton Arms from the 1890s to the 1970s. By the 1940s the business was known simply as Benefit footwear.

Doubleday & Son, 1910. Adjacent to the Clinton Arms Hotel was William Doubleday's ladies' underclothing and baby linen establishment. It is seen here decked out in celebration of the coronation of George V.

Oldhams

Established 1768

CATERERS LTD.

CONFECTIONERS BY ROYAL APPOINTMENT

Wholesale and Retail

𝕭akers and Confectioners

GOLD MEDALLIST

CAFÉ & RESTAURANT

MARKET PLACE
NEWARK
PHONE 168/9

Specialising in Catering for
Private Functions

Advertisement for Oldhams, 1950. The confectionery business of E.E. Oldham and son is still well remembered in the town.

SOME LOST HOUSES
OF NEWARK

Bedlam Lane (right), from the junction of Baldertongate and Cherry Holt Lane (now Sherwood Avenue). The main terraces, to the left and right, were often referred to as the wooden houses on account of the barge boarding evident on their upper storeys. They were demolished in 1910 to make way for the St Leonard's Cottage Homes.

Hardy's Yard, *c*. 1900. A long, narrow thoroughfare, it was one of six so-called yards which connected the Market Place and Stodman Street with Lombard Street. In the early 1900s Hardy's Yard was home to upwards of thirty people.

Portland Street, pre-1937. These homes were demolished in 1937 to make way for the flats of Portland Court. The thoroughfare to the left is Pepper Hill leading to Albert Street opposite Hole's Castle brewery. Today the area between Pepper Hill and the junction of Portland Street and Albert Street is laid out as a small garden.

Barnbygate Lodge, 1933. This charmingly gothic building was located at the corner of Barnbygate and Sherwood Avenue opposite the present tennis courts. The section of Sherwood Avenue which passed beside the house was known as Lodge Lane until it was renamed in 1914. The lodge is thought to have been demolished in about 1934, when the open-air swimming pool was built.

Bede House chapel, Bede House Lane. The chapel, on the left, still stands but the almshouses surrounding it on two sides were demolished in the early 1960s.

The Bedehouses, Bede House Lane. These almshouses were originally endowed by William Phillipot, a wealthy merchant and alderman, in 1556. Constructed initially for the housing of five poor men, they were extended 200 years later in 1756, to accommodate an additional five poor men and five poor women.

Barnbygate. The Methodist church was opened in 1846 and still stands. The corner of the Bedehouses may just be seen on the right. These were demolished in the early 1960s.

Castlegate, looking towards Millgate and Lock Entry.

The so-called Dutch Houses. They were erected on the east side of Millgate in about 1660 and named after their Dutch-style gables. They were said to have been the oldest brick houses in Newark until they were demolished in 1965 to make way for the present Inland Revenue building. This picture is taken from a watercolour painting by E. Ettwell.

Millgate, 1935. Another view of the Dutch Houses (centre left) looking along Millgate towards Pelham Street. Newark Egg Packers (right) were founded in 1931; they later moved to the Wharf (see page 72).

Two views of Water Lane, off Northgate, 1932. Largely demolished during the late 1930s, Water Lane was generally regarded as one of the roughest parts of the town where policemen dared not venture alone.

Regent Street, near Albert Street, 1944. The window above the passageway belonged to 48 Albert Street. The passageway itself gave access to the rear of houses on Regent Street.

Union Terrace, Victoria Street, *c.* 1962. This fine Georgian terrace, with its delicate cast-iron balcony and classical urns, was a sad loss to the architecture of the town when it was demolished in 1967. Part of the site is now occupied by Bishop Alexander Court, which provides sheltered housing for the elderly.

Former toll house, Devon Bridge, Farndon Road. Instead of the usual gate, a heavy chain was said to have been suspended across the road to control access to the turnpiked (improved) section of road.

Magnus Street, looking towards Appletongate, *c*. 1912. Note the trees planted in the road itself (left). Magnus Street was created in 1869 specifically to allow the construction of houses 'suitable for tradesmen or retired persons with limited means'.

Ash's or Queen's Head Yard in the north-west corner of the Market Place, 1928. This photograph illustrates well the appalling state of much of Newark's housing stock before the postwar clearances were commenced.

The Newark Union workhouse, Claypole. A home for some of Newark's less fortunate inhabitants, it was opened in 1817 and closed in 1908. Following subsequent conversion to individual cottage dwellings it was finally demolished in 1978. From a sketch originally published in the *Newark Advertiser* in 1905.

Kirkgate, *c.* 1933. At the door of her shop is Eliza Cobb with Ivy Newbold outside the tobacconist's beyond. This range of buildings was demolished in the late 1930s. The area is now left clear and used as a second-hand car lot.

James Guthrie's house. Once a prominent Newark banker, his house stood on the site now occupied by the Corn Exchange on Castlegate. Built in about 1730, Guthrie's house was demolished in 1847. From a sketch which originally appeared on banknotes issued by Guthrie.

Newark Chantry, Appletongate. Established by Dame Alice Fleming in the fourteenth century it was a residence for the chantry priests of the parish church of St Mary Magdalene. The site is now occupied by the museum and Palace Theatre.

The Chauntry House, Applegate. Alice Fleming's chantry was demolished in the eighteenth century and this fine house erected in its place. This in turn was demolished, in 1920, to make way for the Palace Theatre. Note the similarity between this building and its near contemporary, belonging to James Guthrie, pictured opposite.

The original keeper's lodge, Newark Cemetery, London Road. Dating from 1856 (when the cemetery opened), the lodge has since been superseded by a modern house built on the same site in the 1960s.

Barnbygate House, Barnbygate, *c.* 1906. It was the house of Frederick Henry Appleby JP, surgeon at Newark hospital and a former mayor. The house became the home of Newark Town Club in 1933.

Section Three

NEWARK AT WORK

*The workshop of J. Howitt and Sons, Stodman Street, 1926. Trade directories list
Howitt's as 'furnishing ironmongers, horticultural, agricultural & electrical engineers,
motor & cycle agents & agricultural implement manufacturers'.*

Windmill, London Road, *c*. 1930. Situated on the site now occupied by Woods Court old people's home, the windmill stood in James Smith's timber yard.

Newark millwrights, Messrs Wakes and Lamb, putting up new sails, Coleby Heath mill, Lincolnshire. Founded in 1850, in Parliament Street, the business was sold in 1978 and finally closed in 1985.

Advertisement for Wakes and Lamb, 1897. By the time this advertisement appeared in W.J. Cook's *Directory of Newark*, Wakes & Lamb were well known for their wind-driven pumps, well sinking and pipe laying.

Parnham's water mill (formerly Joseph Thorpe's flour mill) on the Trent. Dating from the eighteenth century, the building was destroyed by fire in 1965 bringing to an end over 130 years of milling by the Parnham family in the town.

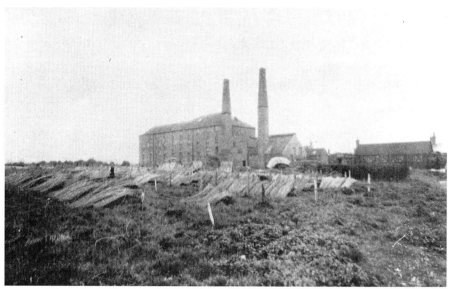

Drying willows, Horace Mills' basket factory, Farndon Road. The factory came to Newark in 1895 and closed in the early 1960s.

Chair-frame shop, Horace Mills' basket factory, 1928. Peeled and dried willow was used to make a variety of chairs, tables, whatnots, settees and all kinds of upholstered goods.

Advertisement, 1897. The finished article: one of Mills' most popular products, the wicker lounge chair. Mills had a local showroom in Middlegate as well as at Birmingham and Glasgow.

The Works of RANSOME & MARLES BEARING Co. Ltd.
NEWARK-on-TRENT, England.

Ransome & Marles' ball-bearing factory, Beacon Hill, *c.* 1935. The firm came to Newark in 1900 and, following a series of takeovers, operates today under the name of NSK-RHP.

The steel stores, Ransome & Marles, Stanley Works, 1930s. Steel bars are being prepared for delivery to the main works where they were ground into ball and roller bearings.

Inspecting the finished ball bearings, Ransome & Marles, 1930s. At this time the only way to ensure that the bearings were free from defect (be it rust cracks or filing marks) was to check each one by hand.

Workers, Ransome & Marles. During the First World War female labour proved invaluable in maintaining required production levels. Third from the left is Hilda Osborne (née Cook).

During the Second World War Ransome & Marles' bearings again proved an essential part of the war effort and were used in almost every instrument of modern warfare.

A machine for producing 'coal eggs'. It was made at W.N. Nicholson's iron foundry, Trentside. Coal eggs were coal dust mixed with cement, and were used as a cheap alternative coal in domestic fires. Kneeling beside the machine is John William Priestley, a foreman.

Advertisement, *c.* 1943. It was in 1919 that Bert Gelsthorpe and Frank Pratt established their motor and electrical engineering business on Baldertongate. During the Second World War they made parts for raising and lowering ailerons on aircraft.

Newark Borough Council's 10-ton steam roller, junction of Magnus Street and Friary Road, 1921.

Advertisement for fly paper, 1912. J.H. Smith began manufacturing his Flydoomo fly papers in Cartergate in the last years of the nineteenth century. By 1912 the business had expanded to such an extent that new premises, the Doomo Works, were established on Lovers' Lane.

The Gilstrap & Earp maltings, Cow Lane. Malting and brewing were once two of Newark's leading industries and were responsible for producing some of the town's most distinctive industrial architecture.

Peach's maltings, Northgate. This is another example of the malting industry's monumental style of architecture. Built in 1881, it became the last working malt kiln in Newark: it closed in September 1980.

Hole's former maltings, Trentside. Not very beautiful perhaps, but this edifice has been identified as a nationally important example of early mass-concrete construction. It is thought to date from between 1877 and 1892.

Two complementary views of malting in Newark. The posed picture (above) shows the tools of the trade, including malt-turning shovels, in use at Thorpe and Sons malting on Millgate. The photograph dates from the First World War, when women supplemented the workforce. For staffing purposes, two females equalled one male worker. The candid shot (below) shows the reality of maltsters working barefoot at Gilstarp, Earp and Co.'s maltings on Northgate. Third from the left is William Allwood.

The first AEC Monarch lorries owned by Gilstrap, Earp and Co., 1937. They are being loaded for delivery.

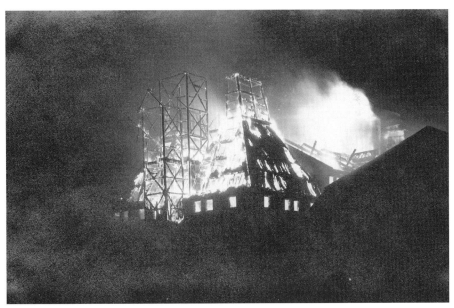

Gilstrap, Earp and Co.'s maltings, Northgate, April 1930. With their large wood content, malt kilns were particularly prone to fire.

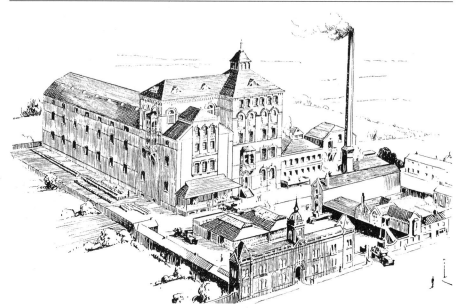

James Hole & Co. Ltd's Castle Brewery, Albert Street. Allied to Newark's malting trade was an equally flourishing brewing industry. The illustration is from a short history of the firm, published in 1935.

Advertisement from the front page, *Newark Advertiser*, 1885. Hole's Castle Brewery became a leading landmark in the town, and for many years the company promoted its interests with prominent advertisements.

Hole's delivery fleet in their yard behind Castle Brewery, Albert Street, mid-1920s. Hole were taken over by the Courage Brewery in 1967.

Warwick and Richardson, brewers, Northgate. Also noted brewers in Newark, they had premises of equal magnitude to those of Hole.

Brewing staff from Warwicks and Richardson's Northgate brewery at Newark Show outside the company's beer tent. The group includes William Pratt.

Warwicks and Richardson's accounts department, 1920s. The secretaries at work are Eileen Lewis (left) and Gladys Hand.

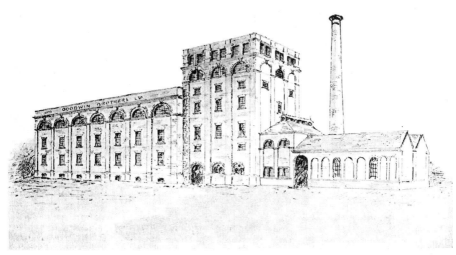

Goodwin Brothers' brewery, 1891. One of Newark's less prominent breweries it later became the Devon Brewery. It was situated between Barnbygate and Baldertongate and opened in 1891.

Workers at W.S. Davy's Devon Brewery (formerly Goodwin Brothers), 1920s. Holding the cask is Thomas William White.

Newark's importance as an agricultural centre is illustrated by the long history of cattle trading in the town. Early fat-stock markets were held on Beastmarket Hill until purpose-built stalls (seen here) were laid out in the castle grounds in 1839.

The cattle market remained in the castle grounds until 1885 when the area was laid out with public walks and pleasure gardens. The Gilstrap Free Library was also built in the grounds in 1883.

Cattle market, Tolney Lane. Following its removal from the castle grounds in 1885, the cattle market was relocated to Tolney Lane where it remained until 1990.

Christmas fat-stock market, Tolney Lane, 1912. The market was of sufficient note (for the high prices raised) to warrant the production of a commemorative postcard. Here the auctioneers Edward Bailey and Son are attending the pig pens.

Beastmarket Hill. Despite the cattle market's relocation to Tolney Lane in 1885, *ad hoc* trading in poultry and game continued on Beastmarket Hill for many years. Indeed it still continues on the Wharf today.

Blagg & Johnson's sheet metal works, Massey Street, 1946. The company was established in 1929 and is still trading successfully today.

Advertisement for George Brown & Son. As well as being monumental masons, this firm was responsible for erecting a good many of Newark's more important early twentieth-century buildings including the post office, Kirkgate in 1908 and the Magnus Grammar School on Earp Avenue in 1909.

Restoration of parish church tower, 1879. This is one of the earliest records of the work of George Brown & Son in Newark. The work was carried out under the guidance of the noted architect G. Gilbert Scott, designer of Kelham Hall and St Pancras station in London.

The basin and wharf along Millgate. Although water transport ultimately failed to compete with the railways, its decline was long and slow. This picture, dating from early this century, shows a still-crowded Trent Navigation. The town's heyday as an inland port had been in the 1880s, when it had regularly handled over 6,500 barges a year.

Southwell Paddy, 1950s. This single-carriage train operated from Rolleston Junction in the 1950s, and connected Southwell with the Newark–Nottingham line. The service was withdrawn in June 1959.

Newark Castle station. The canopy on the Lincoln platform (left) and the water pump (right) have long been removed.

Newark Northgate station, 1950s. Crowds gather to board an excursion train.

CASTLE & SONS,

CARRIAGE and HARNESS MANUFACTURERS,

LOMBARD STREET, NEWARK,

~~~ AND ~~~

VICTORIA SQUARE, WORKSOP.

☞ Patronised by the principal Nobility, Clergy, and Gentry in the County.

Every description of Carriages Built to Order, equal to the First Houses in London

CARRIAGES CAREFULLY WAREHOUSED.

FIRST-CLASS REFERENCES GIVEN.

Carriages of every description may be Purchased on the Three Years Hire System, or LET ON HIRE for any period.

Rubber Tyres fitted to any Wheels.

Electric Light fitted to new or existing Carriages.

Advertisement for Castle & Sons, carriage builders. Serving the nobility of the area, and the numerous coaches that once converged on the town, carriage building in Newark was once an important local industry. Castle & Sons were established in Lombard Street as early as 1812 and continued in business until around 1910 when they finally succumbed to the rise of the motor car.

Lacy's Farm. The farm specialized in growing peas, over an area of up to 60 acres. The site is now occupied by Queen's Court flats, built in 1963. Between about 1810 and the early 1940s the corner of Queen's Road and Appletongate was a stackyard belonging to the farm.

The old Tithe Barn, Lovers' Lane. Also part of Lacy's Farm, the barn was demolished in 1960 and, together with adjacent land, was redeveloped for housing as Tithe Barn Court.

Mr Harold Peet, Tolney Lane. He was a driver for Baxter's livery stables, which was based in the Saracen's Head yard. He is driving part of the company's funeral cortège outside the old bathing place on Tolney Lane.

Newark Egg Packers' fleet of lorries and tricycle outside their premises on the Wharf, c. 1934. Formed in 1931 on Millgate (see page 38), by the time this picture was taken they had expanded into manufacturing pig and poultry food.

Section Four

NEWARK AT PLAY

*Bathing belles at the old bathing place, River Trent, off Tolney Lane. Swimming in the
Trent continued right up to 1934, when the town's open-air swimming pool was built on
Sherwood Avenue.*

Ransome & Marles' works band, 1951. They won their 2000 Guinea Gold Shield at the Belle Vue band contest. Sitting to the left of the shield is Chairman H.P. Thacker, while to the right is Musical Director D. Aspinall.

Jobson's boat house at the mouth of the River Devon. As well as hiring pleasure craft to local day-trippers, Bert Jobson also traded as a boat builder.

CASTLE BREWERY OFFICES

Just a card from friends in Newark,
With this message, they have sent,
T'would do you good to visit here,
And stroll beside the River Trent.

Or take a trip in "Jobson's" launch,
On this fine water-way;
It would revive, and do such good,
You'd feel inclined to stay.

Then quench your thirst with Newark Ale,
A wholesome beverage, brewed
From water, malt,
and hops combined.
You'll then go
home renewed.

THE BOATING STATION

Bert Jobson's boating station immortalized on a Newark greetings card.

First Newark Girls Friendly Society weekend camp, Winthorpe, July 1928.

Newark, Winthorpe and Collingham Girl Guides, 1 August 1928. They are heading for their summer camp at Flamborough. On the far left, standing beside the charabanc, is Gwen Maltby.

Broadway Hotel. Little changed today, except in ownership, the hotel was opened by the Newark brewing firm, Warwicks and Richardson's, on Bowbridge Road in December 1939.

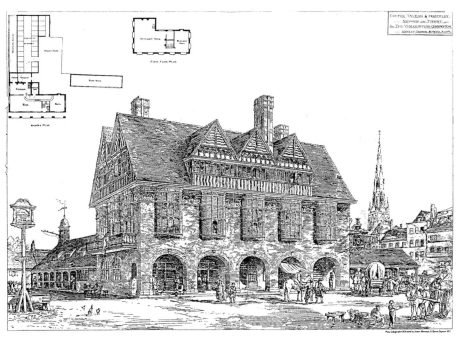

Ossington Coffee Palace, 1882. It was given to Newark by Viscountess Ossington of Ossington Hall who was concerned about the amount of alcohol consumed by farmers on market days. The coffee palace, opened in November 1882, was her attempt to attract farmers away from the demon drink. It never completely succeeded.

The Ram Hotel, Castlegate. It was one of Newark's eleven or so coaching inns: note the central arch which gave vehicle access to the yard behind. The building is believed to date from the 1770s.

The Ram Hotel trade card, 1930s. The Ram's coaching arch has been converted into the main entrance. The configuration persists to this day.

The Ram Hotel trade card, 1930s. This resplendent entrance hall took the place of the old coach arch seen on the engraving opposite.

The Ram Hotel winter garden, 1930s. G.H. Ducksbury was proprietor and licensee from the mid-1930s until the hotel was purchased by the Home Brewery of Nottingham in 1939.

The Castle and Falcon, London Road. First mentioned in 1788, much of it was rebuilt in about 1813 with stabling for seventy horses. The caption claims that William Ewart Gladstone (whose first parliamentary seat from 1832 was for Newark) made his first speech from this pub. It was actually made from the Clinton Arms, in the Market Place.

The White Hind (now the Zoo), Cartergate, May 1937. A pub of this name was mentioned on the site as long ago as 1796. Here it is seen decorated for the coronation of King George VI.

The Blue Man. The earliest known reference to the Blue Man public house on Northgate dates from 1832; the pub is still going strong today. It was formerly one of the houses tied to the local Warwicks and Richardson's brewery.

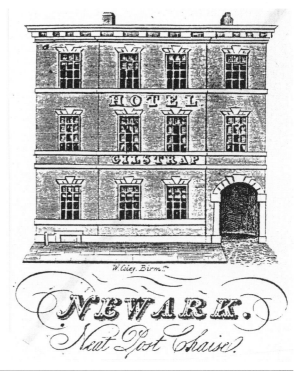

The Hotel, Kirkgate. Another of Newark's once thriving coaching inns, it was bought by Joseph Gilstrap in 1818 and run by him until its closure in 1853; the expanding rail network had all but killed the coaching trade. The building is now occupied by the Black Horse estate agency. This illustration comes from a billhead used by the hotel in the early 1800s.

The Northern Hotel (latterly the Bowling Green), opposite Newark's Northgate railway station. It was created out of two or three cottages in the mid-1860s and extensively modernized in 1934, when this photograph was taken.

The Midland Hotel, close to Newark's castle railway station. It was built in 1886 and originally intended to offer short-stay accommodation for businesmen using the railway. It is still trading today.

Out for a spin, *c*. 1913. Sitting on the bonnet is Tom Postil; Nancy Postil is seated nearest to the camera. They were of the Postil family who ran a boot and shoe shop at 6 Bridge Street. The others are members of the Knight family of grocers.

FRED CROWSON

F. J. CROWSON

—

DOVEDALE
FARNDON ROAD
NEWARK-NOTTS.

'Forces'
Choice

ENSURE THE SUCCESS OF THE

PARTY or CONCERT YOU ARE PLANNING

BY ADDING MAGIC TO THE ENTERTAINMENT.

PROGRAMMES FOR ALL OCCASIONS

Advertisement for a conjurer, 1950. Newark had a small band of entertainers who could be relied upon to brighten up any party or entertainment being staged in the town.

Newark May Fair, *c*. 1911. The fair was traditionally held in the Market Place, as seen here, but later moved to a paddock on London Road and thence to Tolney Lane.

Flooding at a fair, Tolney Lane, *c*. 1933. A challenge boxing booth may be seen among the stranded caravans at the far left.

Newark Amateur Operatic Society Palace Theatre, 1938. Formed in 1936, this is a scene from their first production, Gilbert and Sullivan's *The Gondoliers*.

Pageant of Newark, 13–18 July 1936. Over the years Newark Castle grounds have been used as the setting for many theatrical events. One of the largest was this pageant in which over 2,000 local people were involved. The entire cast is seen here assembled for the finale.

For seven nights during June and July 1971 the Newark Amateur Operatic Society augmented a professional cast, including Donald Adams and Thomas Round, for a production of Gilbert and Sullivan's *The Mikado*. The production was highly acclaimed and, as this picture shows, well attended.

Carl Welham, the Green Man. In July 1992 the castle grounds were used as the venue for a new community play tracing the history of Newark from earliest times. *The Leaves of Life* was written by Nottingham playwright Michael Eaton.

One of the most memorable scenes from *The Leaves of Life*, July 1992. Two cooks, Steve Watson (left) and Harry Keeling, assisted by pageboy Philip Whitaker, prepare a meal for King John prior to his visit to Newark Castle in October 1216.

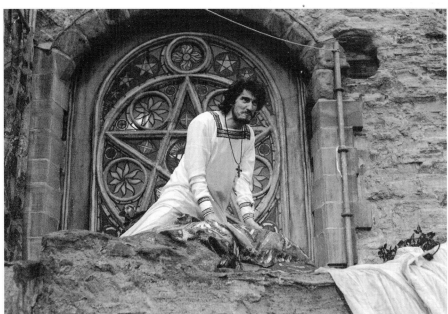

King John (Glen Kinch), *The Leaves of Life*, July 1992. Over 200 local people were involved in the play's production. They were supported by the professional skill of the Major Road Theatre Co. of Bradford and the Nottingham Playhouse.

The new year's meet of the South Notts. Hunt, Market Place, 10 January 1955. On horseback is Capt. Tom Bayley (joint Master), while the Mayor, Coun. G. Walker, drinks the health of the hunt. Town Clerk, J.H.M. Greaves (right) pauses as one of the hounds jumps up.

R101 airship over Newark, October 1929. Crowds lined the streets to see this, its second flight. This photograph was taken by local chimney sweep Freddie Fenton of George Street from near the River Trent.

Newark's annual Sunday school festival. It was held on the third Thursday (later Saturday) in June. Floats, or 'devices', created by different Sunday schools around the town, were judged and awarded prizes according to their splendour and inventiveness.

Charles Street Wesleyan School device, Newark Sunday school festival, 1909. It is a replica of The Regent stage coach which once plied between Peterborough and Newark.

Sunday school festival device. Also produced by the Charles Street Wesleyan School it shows the elaborate detail which could be achieved.

Sconce Hills, 1932. After parading around the town with their devices and having tea, those involved in the Sunday school festival would make their way to Sconce Hills for further entertainments. Here, children from Newark Baptist church perform their action song, 'Nursery Rhymes'.

Members of the Sunday school, United Methodist (or Methodist New Connection) chapel, Barnbygate, *c.* 1918–20. Standing on the left (front) is Charlotte Heath.

Interior, Barnbygate Methodist chapel. Opened in 1846, it was situated almost directly opposite the New Connection chapel shown above. It is presumed that this picture commemmorates the ending of the First World War.

Newark from Tolney Lane. This early postcard, published by Samuel Whiles of Newark, shows many of the town's principal landmarks: the castle, the parish church of St Mary, the Corn Exchange and the wooden haleing bridge. The latter, built in about 1827, carried the Trent Navigation towpath over the Mill Race.

Newark Castle, as depicted in an engraving published in 1816 at the height of the coaching era.

Newark Castle grounds, *c.* 1890. The grounds were opened in May 1889 and inhabited by peacocks, as depicted in this engraving published by Samuel Whiles.

The Undercroft. Sometimes erroneously referred to as the crypt, this lies beneath the castle terrace. It is thought the undercroft was originally used either as a store or a servants' hall.

A somewhat fanciful impression of the undercroft at Newark Castle. Drawn by W.H. Cable, and published in 1838, this engraving formed the frontispiece to *The Midland Counties Literary Repository* of that year.

Russian cannon, Newark Castle. For many years this 36-lb Russian cannon was positioned on the terrace within the castle grounds, pointing out over the Trent. The gun was captured from the Russians at Sebastopol in 1855 and presented to the town in 1857.

First World War short-barrelled mortar, also positioned on the castle terrace for many years. Both the Russian cannon and the mortar were removed in 1942 when their metal was required for salvage to assist the war effort.

First World War tank, Castlegate, 13 August 1919. Between 1919 and 1936 Newark's castle grounds were adorned by a First World War tank presented to the town in recognition of its financial contribution to the war effort. Here the tank is making its triumphal entrance along Castlegate.

Section Five

SOME MORE SHOPS

Brush shop, 55 (now 61) Appletongate, c. 1882. It belonged to Robert Wilkinson (second left). Brushes were made on the premises – hence the large workforce – and sold widely to chimney sweeps, the council, and for domestic use.

Henry Clark with his wife, Henrietta, *c.* 1920s. He was a fish and rabbit dealer and lived in Lawrence Street. Fish, collected from Northgate station, was sold by the Clarks on their market stall.

James Hudson's fish stall. Left to right: Hilda Hudson (James' daughter), James and his wife Rose (née Clark). James Hudson joined the Clarks' fish business through his marriage to Henry Clark's daughter, Rose. The family firm still trades in the Market Place today, as Jackie's fish stall.

William Hefford Bailey's drapery shop, 2 Barnbygate. In local trade directories of 1885 Bailey is listed as draper's assistant elsewhere in the town, although by 1892 he had opened his own shop on Barnbygate. Here he continued until about 1910. His private residence was at 58 Harcourt Street. The Barnbygate premises now house a card shop.

Ann J. Campbell's drapery and millinery shop, 5 Kirkgate. It is probably best remembered, during the 1930s and 1940s, as located in the Market Hall behind the Town Hall. Before that, however, she ran her business at Kirkgate. Mrs Campbell is pictured in the doorway.

Imperial Buildings, junction of Baldertongate and Barnbygate with Appletongate, 1944. They were built in the eighteenth century and have since been occupied by some of the town's most successful businesses. Seen here are the businesses of George Mason (grocer) and Ernest Randall (outfitter).

George Mason's grocery store, *c.* 1936. Two of his assistants, J. Warriner (left) and Sid Yarnell pose outside. Mason occupied a position in Imperial Buildings for approximately fifty years between about 1910 and 1954.

Ernest Randall's, 1930s. He began his long association with Imperial Buildings on 18 June 1902 when he opened his first shop in a small lock-up on the Baldertongate side of the building. By the 1930s, however, the business had expanded considerably into neighbouring premises.

Ernest Thomas Hall Randall (1878–53), photographed in 1944. In this year he was president of the Newark Tradesmen's Association. As well as founding his successful retailing business, Mr Randall was a town councillor and mayor in 1946.

Randall's, workroom, Baldertongate, 1930s. By the 1930s Randall's was employing no fewer than ten tailors who worked in rooms above the Baldertongate shop frontage. Some are seen here working in traditional style sitting cross-legged on the cutting table

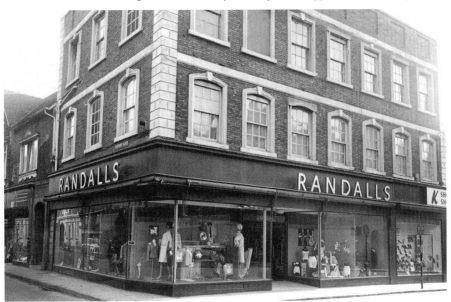

Randall's Imperial Buildings, 1950s. By this time Randall's had expanded to such an extent that the shop occupied the whole of Imperial Buildings, presenting an uninterrupted frontage to three of the most important retailing streets in the town. The business continued in this location until the 1960s when it moved across the road to 3 Appletongate.

TWENTY-ONE WINDOW DISPLAYS IN
THREE STREETS, OF CURRENT FASHIONS
FOR MEN, LADIES AND CHILDREN,
LAYETTES AND BABYWEAR, HOUSE-
HOLD GOODS, FURNISHING FABRICS,
RUG AND KNITTING WOOLS, ETC.,
BY ALL THE LEADING MAKERS

Newark's Department Store
Established Over Half a Century

Imperial Buildings, Baldertongate
Bridge Street, Barnbygate, Newark

Telephone 111

Advertisement for Randall's outfitters, 1957. The well-known logo is still in use today.

Stodman Street, looking towards the Market Place, *c*. 1900. Richard Blagg's butchers shop is on the corner of Middlegate (left).

The Quality Furniture store, 18–20 Barnbygate, 1950. The shop occupied premises previously owned by the Devon Brewery (see page 63).

Castlegate, looking towards Beastmarket Hill, 1910. The building on the right was occupied by the Stamford, Spalding and Boston Bank. The site was later taken over by Lloyds Bank (see below).

Lloyds Bank, corner of Castlegate and Stodman Street, 1956. The building was new that year – a great improvement for traffic as it was set back from the road.

Knight's grocery and confectionery shop, corner of Appletongate and Barnbygate, *c*. 1908. Alex Knight moved into the premises between 1885 and 1888 and continued on the site until about 1932.

Knight, Dickins & Co., 1–3 Appletongate. By 1936 Knight's had merged with A. Dickins and Co. The business continued trading until October 1966.

For Quality
and Service

WE DELIVER WITHIN
A RADIUS OF
12 MILES

KNIGHT, DICKINS & C̥°LTD

GROCERIES & PROVISIONS · KNIGHT, DICKINS & C°LTD · WINES & SPIRTS · BASS

High-Class Grocers Provision Wine & Spirit Merchants
APPLETON GATE NEWARK

Bottlers of
HARP LABEL
Guinness

Advertisement for Knight, Dickins & Co., 1957.

FAMOUS

FOR

MEN'S WEAR

OF

QUALITY

R. J. HAMBLING

HIGH CLASS TAILOR & OUTFITTER

29 Stodman St., Newark

Tel. 33

Advertisement for Hambling, tailor. The tailoring business on Stodman Street, now owned by R.J. Hambling, may be traced back as far as 1795.

'Hats through the ages', Hambling display, 1936. The display was mounted in Hambling's window to coincide with the historical 'Pageant of Newark' staged in the castle grounds in 1936 (see page 85).

Advertisement for Hambling, 1942. Hambling offered a complete tailoring service to the military in wartime.

Taylor's Drug Co., chemist shop, 9 Cartergate, 1935. Later that decade the shop became a branch of Timothy White's. A chemist shop continued on the site until 1977.

The Governor's House, Stodman Street, 1930s. At this time it was divided into two shops: Ernest Rick the tailors (left) and Lees and Sons, tobacconists.

J. Pratt's fish and game shop, opposite the Arcade, Cartergate, early 1900s. On the far right is John Pratt, the owner, with his wife.

I'm pleased to see you again Mr. Wearer

—says Mr. Weaver.

3 SPECIALITIES:

Raincoats - - **16 9**
(TRIPLE-PROOFED)

Sports Coats - **16 -**
(ALL WOOL)

Flannel Trousers - **5 -**

All-Wool Serge
SUIT
or Art Silk Lined
OVERCOAT
30/-

WEAVER TO WEARER LTD.

Mr. Wearer : I am glad to come back, Mr. Weaver. I have been having a good look round but I have not found anything to beat your values yet.

Mr. Weaver : I should think it would be difficult. Our enormous turnover enables us to put many an extra ounce of value into our suits, and it is this which makes them head and shoulders above the crowd.

Mr. Wearer : Well I am relying on you to fix me up with something extra smart.

Mr. Weaver : There are 500 cloths for you to choose from, and whatever your taste, I am sure you will be satisfied.

Advertisement for Weaver's, 1936. When Weaver's placed this advertisement they were new to the town; they continued trading in Newark until the 1950s.

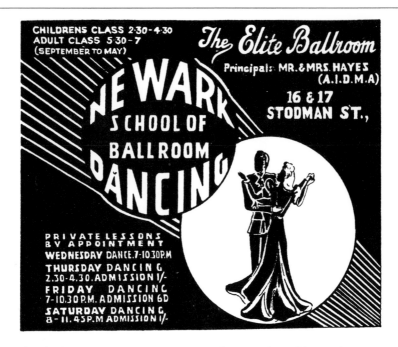

Dance-school advertisements, *c.* 1942. During the Second World War dances were held regularly at the Corn Exchange, Town Hall and the Beaumond Chambers. Newark boasted no fewer than five separate dance schools.

Kirkgate, *c.* 1908. The newly opened post office is on the right.

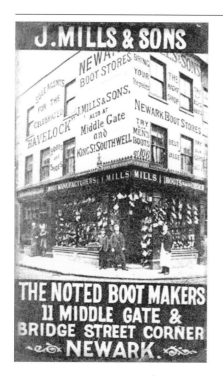

John Mills & Sons, corner of Bridge Street and Appletongate, early 1900s.

JOHN MILLS & SONS, LTD.

Newark   Bakewell
Hinckley   Southwell

The Largest
SOLID LEATHER BOOT
In the World

*The "Big Boot" Shop
for Big Value*

Although well regarded as a shoe salesman, for many the overriding memory of Mills' shop in Middlegate was the world's largest leather boot, which was displayed prominently in the window. It was made in 1887 for the Newark Tradesmen's procession at Queen Victoria's Golden Jubilee celebrations.

Advertisement for Mills' shop, 1897. Mills continued trading in the town until the mid-1960s.

Melias grocery shop, 28 Stodmand Street. It was a feature in Newark from the 1920s through to the mid-1960s.

H. Clarke's café and the Meadow Dairy, 1944. They shared the building at 37 Stodman Street. Despite its name the Meadow Dairy is listed in trade directories as a general provisions store.

Advertisements for Ena Porter's women's outfitters, 1950. Ena Porter's ('art needlework, ladies' gowns, wools, silks and lingerie') may be seen as the spiritual successor to Madame Cooke (see page 17).

Boots, 1949. The Nottingham firm of Boots opened its shop in Newark in the mid-1890s and still occupies the same Stodman Street site today.

J.T. Covell's fish and poultry shop, corner of Kirkgate and Bar Gate, 1933. The site is now occupied by the New King Wah Chinese restaurant.

Section Six

THE GREAT AND THE GOOD

Cornelius Brown. Probably Newark's most distinguished local historian, his seminal History of Newark, *published in two volumes, 1904 and 1907, remains the most complete study of the town's distinguished past. Brown was editor of the* Newark Advertiser *for thirty-three years. He died in October 1907, just days before the second volume of his history was published.*

William Gilstrap. In 1883 he endowed the town with its first free public library (see page 64). Gilstrap was head of the prominent local malting firm of Gilstrap, Earp & Co. (see page 56) and was later knighted for his numerous charitable acts.

Arthur Smith. Newark's best-remembered chief librarian at the Gilstrap Library, he held the post for no fewer than forty-one years, 1919–60.

Jessie Bond. One of the original performers of Gilbert and Sullivan's operas at the Savoy Theatre in London, Jessie Bond became a resident of Farndon near Newark in 1900. She came to Newark as the wife of Lewis Ransome, a director of A. Ransome and Co. – later Ransome & Marle and now NSK-RHP (see page 52).

Nat Gould (1857–1919). He wrote over 130 novels and, in his day, was one of the country's most popular authors. Although born in Cheshire it was in Newark that he gained his literary training on the staff of the *Newark Advertiser*, from 1878 to 1884.

Lord Byron. In 1806 the first collection of poems to be published by Lord Byron was printed in Newark. Entitled *Fugitive Pieces* only two copies of that original imprint are thought to survive. This portrait of Byron, preserved at Newstead Abbey his ancestral home, was painted in 1814 by Thomas Phillips.

The printing press upon which Byron's first poems are said to have been printed. The press is now preserved in Newark museum.

Byron's first poems were printed by the firm of S. & J. Ridge, whose premises in the Market Place are today occupied by G.H. Porter's grocery shop (see page 22). While overseeing the printing of his poems, Bryon is said to have stayed at the Clinton Arms Hotel across the Market Place.

W.E. Gladstone. Another figure of national importance associated with Newark is W.E. Gladstone. Gladstone was first elected to the House of Commons as Member for Newark in 1832. He went on to become a noted statesman and four times prime minister.

Lieut. Gonville Bromhead (1845–91). He was one of the most famous pupils to attend the Magnus Grammar School in Newark. During the Zulu Wars, in 1879, he was awarded the VC for his part in the battle of Rorke's Drift in defence of Natal. In the film *Zulu* (1964) he was played by Michael Caine.

Robert Kiddey (1900–84). The Nottingham-born artist and sculptor was, for many years, a teacher at the Newark Technical College. During the 1930s his work was exhibited alongside that of Picasso and Eric Gill. He is pictured here in his studio at 5 King Street, Newark, with a relief carving in wood called 'Crucifixion'.

Sir Godfrey Hounsfield (left), receiving the Nobel prize for Physiology/Medicine from King Gustav of Sweden, December 1979. The Newark-born scientist invented the brain scanner, now used in hospitals across the world.

Kate Greenaway (1846–1901). The world-renowned children's author and illustrator spent much time in her childhood at the village of Rolleston near Newark. The scenery of Nottinghamshire formed an important influence on many of Greenaway's adult paintings.

Acknowledgements

I wish to express my sincere thanks to the following, without whom the production of this book would not have been possible: Miss J.M. Antoine, for permission to reproduce photographs from original negatives taken by her father, Mr N.J. Antoine, in the thirties and forties; Roy Wells, for access to his extensive collection of photographs and postcards which, together with those of Miss Antoine, form the backbone of this compilation; Mr M. Gill and Ruth Petersen, for reading and offering comments on an earlier draft of the book; and Mr Rupert Vinnicombe, Newark District Librarian, for his support and encouragement.

Finally, thanks to those many individuals who have granted me permission to use photographs from their private collections:

Mr D.E. Arundel • Mr P. Beaumont • Mrs V. Brittain • Mr H. Brown
Mr P.J. Burke • Mrs J. Carter • Mrs A. Chester • Mrs E.M. Clark
Mr M. Clark • Mr W.F. Coyne • Mr M. Gill • Mrs M. Glenn
Mr C.R.W. Grant • Mr T. Healey • Mrs R. Holmes • Sir G. Hounsfield KT
Miss M. Hounsfield • Mr R.L. Hutchinson • Mrs M. Kelly • Mr J.T. Kirk
Mr J. Knight • Mrs M. Lancaster • Mrs B. Mackinder
Midland Railway Trust • Newstead Abbey (Nottingham City Council)
Mrs A.E. Parker • Mr R. Parker • Dr S. Pawley • Mrs A. Priestley
Mr J.M. Randall • Mr B. Robb • Mr F.M. Rouse • Mrs G.A. Spiers
Mr R.W. Town • Mr S.A. Vanns • Mr J. Warriner • Mr B. Webb
Mrs E. Welthorpe • Mr B. White • Mr F.H. Yeomans

BRITAIN IN OLD PHOTOGRAPHS

To order any of these titles please telephone Littlehampton Book Services on 01903 721596

Scunthorpe, *D Taylor*
Skegness, *W Kime*
Around Skegness, *W Kime*

LONDON

Balham and Tooting, *P Loobey*
Crystal Palace, Penge & Anerley, *M Scott*
Greenwich and Woolwich, *K Clark*
Hackney: A Second Selection, *D Mander*
Lewisham and Deptford, *J Coulter*
Lewisham and Deptford: A Second Selection, *J Coulter*
Streatham, *P Loobey*
Around Whetstone and North Finchley, *J Heathfield*
Woolwich, *B Evans*

MONMOUTHSHIRE

Chepstow and the River Wye, *A Rainsbury*
Monmouth and the River Wye, *Monmouth Museum*

NORFOLK

Great Yarmouth, *M Teun*
Norwich, *M Colman*
Wymondham and Attleborough, *P Yaxley*

NORTHAMPTONSHIRE

Around Stony Stratford, *A Lambert*

NOTTINGHAMSHIRE

Arnold and Bestwood, *M Spick*
Arnold and Bestwood: A Second Selection, *M Spick*
Changing Face of Nottingham, *G Oldfield*
Mansfield, *Old Mansfield Society*
Around Newark, *T Warner*
Nottingham: 1944–1974, *D Whitworth*
Sherwood Forest, *D Ottewell*
Victorian Nottingham, *M Payne*

OXFORDSHIRE

Around Abingdon, *P Horn*
Banburyshire, *M Barnett & S Gosling*
Burford, *A Jewell*
Around Didcot and the Hagbournes, *B Lingham*
Garsington, *M Gunther*
Around Henley-on-Thames, *S Ellis*
Oxford: The University, *J Rhodes*
Thame to Watlington, *N Hood*
Around Wallingford, *D Beasley*
Witney, *T Worley*
Around Witney, *C Mitchell*
Witney District, *T Worley*
Around Woodstock, *J Bond*

POWYS

Brecon, *Brecknock Museum*
Welshpool, *E Bredsdorff*

SHROPSHIRE

Shrewsbury, *D Trumper*
Whitchurch to Market Drayton, *M Morris*

SOMERSET

Bath, *J Hudson*
Bridgwater and the River Parrett, *R Fitzhugh*
Bristol, *D Moorcroft & N Campbell-Sharp*
Changing Face of Keynsham,
   B Lowe & M Whitehead

Chard and Ilminster, *G Gosling & F Huddy*
Crewkerne and the Ham Stone Villages,
   G Gosling & F Huddy
Around Keynsham and Saltford, *B Lowe & T Brown*
Midsomer Norton and Radstock, *C Howell*
Somerton, Ilchester and Langport, *G Gosling & F Huddy*
Taunton, *N Chipchase*
Around Taunton, *N Chipchase*
Wells, *C Howell*
Weston-Super-Mare, *S Poole*
Around Weston-Super-Mare, *S Poole*
West Somerset Villages, *K Houghton & L Thomas*

STAFFORDSHIRE

Aldridge, *J Farrow*
Bilston, *E Rees*
Black Country Transport: Aviation, *A Brew*
Around Burton upon Trent, *G Sowerby & R Farman*
Bushbury, *A Chatwin, M Mills & E Rees*
Around Cannock, *M Mills & S Belcher*
Around Leek, *R Poole*
Lichfield, *H Clayton & K Simmons*
Around Pattingham and Wombourne, *M Griffiths,*
   P Leigh & M Mills
Around Rugeley, *T Randall & J Anslow*
Smethwick, *J Maddison*
Stafford, *J Anslow & T Randall*
Around Stafford, *J Anslow & T Randall*
Stoke-on-Trent, *I Lawley*
Around Tamworth, *R Sulima*
Around Tettenhall and Codsall, *M Mills*
Tipton, Wednesbury and Darlaston, *R Pearson*
Walsall, *D Gilbert & M Lewis*
Wednesbury, *I Bott*
West Bromwich, *R Pearson*

SUFFOLK

Ipswich: A Second Selection, *D Kindred*
Around Ipswich, *D Kindred*
Around Mildenhall, *C Dring*
Southwold to Aldeburgh, *H Phelps*
Around Woodbridge, *H Phelps*

SURREY

Cheam and Belmont, *P Berry*
Croydon, *S Bligh*
Dorking and District, *K Harding*
Around Dorking, *A Jackson*
Around Epsom, *P Berry*
Farnham: A Second Selection, *J Parratt*
Around Haslemere and Hindhead, *T Winter & G Collyer*
Richmond, *Richmond Local History Society*
Sutton, *P Berry*

SUSSEX

Arundel and the Arun Valley, *J Godfrey*
Bishopstone and Seaford, *P Pople & P Berry*
Brighton and Hove, *J Middleton*
Brighton and Hove: A Second Selection, *J Middleton*
Around Crawley, *M Goldsmith*
Hastings, *P Haines*
Hastings: A Second Selection, *P Haines*
Around Haywards Heath, *J Middleton*
Around Heathfield, *A Gillet & B Russell*
Around Heathfield: A Second Selection,
   A Gillet & B Russell
High Weald, *B Harwood*
High Weald: A Second Selection, *B Harwood*
Horsham and District, *T Wales*

Lewes, *J Middleton*
RAF Tangmere, *A Saunders*
Around Rye, *A Dickinson*
Around Worthing, *S White*

WARWICKSHIRE

Along the Avon from Stratford to Tewkesbury, *J Jeremiah*
Bedworth, *J Burton*
Coventry, *D McGrory*
Around Coventry, *D McGrory*
Nuneaton, *S Clews & S Vaughan*
Around Royal Leamington Spa, *J Cameron*
Around Royal Leamington Spa: A Second Selection,
   J Cameron
Around Warwick, *R Booth*

WESTMORLAND

Eden Valley, *J Marsh*
Kendal, *M & P Duff*
South Westmorland Villages, *J Marsh*
Westmorland Lakes, *J Marsh*

WILTSHIRE

Around Amesbury, *P Daniels*
Chippenham and Lacock, *A Wilson & M Wilson*
Around Corsham and Box, *A Wilson & M Wilson*
Around Devizes, *D Buxton*
Around Highworth, *G Tanner*
Around Highworth and Faringdon, *G Tanner*
Around Malmesbury, *A Wilson*
Marlborough: A Second Selection, *P Colman*
Around Melksham,
   Melksham and District Historical Association
Nadder Valley, *R. Sawyer*
Salisbury, *P Saunders*
Salisbury: A Second Selection, *P Daniels*
Salisbury: A Third Selection, *P Daniels*
Around Salisbury, *P Daniels*
Swindon: A Third Selection, *The Swindon Society*
Swindon: A Fourth Selection, *The Swindon Society*
Trowbridge, *M Marshman*
Around Wilton, *P Daniels*
Around Wootton Bassett, Cricklade and Purton, *T Sharp*

WORCESTERSHIRE

Evesham to Bredon, *F Archer*
Around Malvern, *K Smith*
Around Pershore, *M Dowty*
Redditch and the Needle District, *R Saunders*
Redditch: A Second Selection, *R Saunders*
Around Tenbury Wells, *D Green*
Worcester, *M Dowty*
Around Worcester, *R Jones*
Worcester in a Day, *M Dowty*
Worcestershire at Work, *R Jones*

YORKSHIRE

Huddersfield: A Second Selection, *H Wheeler*
Huddersfield: A Third Selection, *H Wheeler*
Leeds Road and Rail, *R Vickers*
Pontefract, *R van Riel*
Scarborough, *D Coggins*
Scarborough's War Years, *R Percy*
Skipton and the Dales, *Friends of the Craven Museum*
Around Skipton-in-Craven, *Friends of the Craven Museum*
Yorkshire Wolds, *I & M Sumner*